NYC
Tarot

Bess Matassa

AF129957

with art by Clara Kirkpatrick

STERLING ETHOS
New York

STERLING ETHOS
New York

Text © 2023 Bess Matassa
Art © 2023 Clara Kirkpatrick

ISBN 978-1-4549-4919-0

For information about custom editions,
special sales, and premium purchases, please contact
specialsales@unionsquareandco.com.

Manufactured in China

2 4 6 8 10 9 7 5 3 1

unionsquareandco.com

Cover and interior design by Stacy Wakefield Forte

Introduction

THERE ARE SEVENTY-EIGHT SECONDS in every New York minute, and this tarot deck is a magical way for you to celebrate them. Toss your deck and let each card rain down like New Year's ball-drop confetti as you welcome this unstoppable city's wildness into your life with palms spread wide. All you've got to do is shuffle up, take to the concrete, and just say yes to whatever energies cross your path.

You cannot spend one second in this city without becoming more alive. It is a physical and psychic impossibility. And the tarot is no different; each of the cards in your pack is forever longing to spring forth with saturated life, sparked by a simple touch from your fingertips. To come to your deck is always an opportunity to come to *more* life, embracing the full menu of humanness without turning away from any flavor that's being served.

Far from a prognostic future oracle that divines your destiny, this tarot, like the town that inspired it, asks for your participation in each card pull. You can think of your deck as a kind of psychic subway system that powers beneath your conscious mind. Sometimes you'll pull a card and nod your head and heart with deep knowing—assured that what you've been feeling on the interior has now come out to play in pictorial form. In other moments, you might get a little surprise as a card offers a new way of traveling through and making sense of your situation. To ask questions of your deck is to commune with your many selves: the multitudes that teem through the urban topography that is you.

This city encompasses all of it and holds nothing back. And your *NYC Tarot* wants you to hold all of it, too. From the Yonkers border on down to the Staten Island sea; and from the bridge-and-tunnels of Jersey all the way to the briny Montauk end. Spread your cards wide and stack 'em as high as the skyscrapers reaching into the sky. Because—after all—if you can make magic here, you can make it anywhere.

The Keys to the City: Insider Tips for Unlocking Your Deck

The Card Triptych

 OUR DECK IS COMPOSED of three categories of cards, which each offer up a distinctive stripe of sensation.

THE MAJOR ARCANA: BIG APPLES. The twenty-one cards of the Major Arcana (plus the Fool) represent the most iconic of human happenings—those soul-changing evolutions that so many of us encounter during our lives. In this deck, they're symbolized by quintessential New York locales and experiences. Likewise, you can treat their energies like immersive environments, getting curious about their emotional contexts and taking a wander through their worlds.

THE MINOR ARCANA: STREET SYMPHONIES. The Minors are our moment-to-moment cards: the street-level, on-the-ground experiences of everyday living. The forty cards that make up their cosmic crew are divided into four suits of ten, which carry the vibration of the four elements (fire, water, air, earth) that make up all of existence:

WANDS (FIRE): FIRE ESCAPES. Fire welcomes us to the Broadway-jazz-hands sensations of life. This suit asks us to explore themes of willpower, self-expression, participation, and fundamental, open-fire-hydrant life force.

CUPS (WATER): TO-GO CUPS. Water welcomes us to the sea-swept sensitivities of a city awash with emotion. This suit asks us to explore themes of tending and mending, lovability, release, and primal pulls and patterns.

SWORDS (AIR): THE SUBWAY SYSTEM. Air welcomes us to the circulating engine of the city and the willingness to travel into new realms. This suit asks us to explore themes of perception, spaciousness, energy exchange, and consciousness shifts.

PENTACLES (EARTH): PIZZA PIES. Earth welcomes us to the sensual experience of a city with everything on offer. This suit asks us to explore themes of internal resources, worthiness, self-sufficiency, and soul security.

THE COURT CARDS: NATIVE NEW YORKERS. Each of these sixteen cards is here to help us "be." If you're arriving to the city as a voyager, you can imagine that they're different outfits safely stored in your suitcase. And if you're a longtime resident, they're the sweaters tucked into your apartment closet (plus a few pairs of shoes in the oven if you're living in a studio). Just as New York gives us the opportunity to reinvent and remember all the parts of us, you can practice making each of these cards a part of you and trying on its way of walking through the world.

THE PAGES: STREET SNACKS. These cards offer us the chance to freshen up and add some pep to our step. We can use them to reinvigorate our sense of innocence, hope, and newness.

THE KNIGHTS: CITY CROSSINGS. These cards invite us to let more life *through* us, as we learn to meet situations with an adaptable spirit. We can use them to respond to shifting rhythms.

THE QUEENS: URBAN OASES. These cards are the gate-keepers of our inner sanctums. We can use them to commune with the private altars inside of us that no one can ever alter.

THE KINGS: HIGH-RISES. These cards are the space takers and makers, here to remind us of the force of our footprint. We can use them to settle into easeful ownership over our lives.

Card Meanings

EACH OF THE TAROT'S seventy-eight cards puts forth a powerful proposition. When you pull one from the pack, it's an invitation to explore where its meaning might live inside your soul in this moment, and to get curious about how you might let it lift you. No card ever wants to hurt you, punish you, or fix your destiny in Manhattan schist. All of them are here to help you flourish. The card meanings in this guidebook are intended to spark your own musings—just as a city guidebook would lead you to a locale and suggest hot tips.

Learning your deck means learning to live it. Each card in this guidebook also offers up some personal inquiry questions and suggestions for exploring its energies out in the world. Let these sections inspire you toward adventures of your own as you treasure-hunt for "evidence" of each card's symbolic resonance, wherever you are. If you're in NYC, you might even use these tips to plan your day's magical itinerary: pulling a few cards and then setting off to explore their sites.

Reversals

Some tarot readers work with what are termed "reversals" and interpret distinctive meanings when a card arrives "upside down" instead of "right side up" during a pull. In this guidebook, you'll find only one meaning for each card. This is inspired by the belief that we come to the tarot, just as we come to the city, from a multitude of emotional and energetic angles that transcend the binary of upright versus downturned. You're encouraged to use the singular meaning that's given as a launchpad to explore your own personal orientation to a given card. Sometimes you'll "come at" a card's meaning sideways through sliding subway-car doors, slipping inside with a sigh of relief as you're whisked on your way. Other times, you might resist a card's pull like you're racing backward trying to break free from a Times Square throng. There is no right or wrong way to show up to the teachings of any given card, only an invitation to see where you are in your meet-and-greet with its energies. Let yourself explore this approach to a given card without worrying about the direction of the picture.

Shuffling + Spreading

If you're in the Naked City right now, take a moment to peep outside and notice all the ways your neighbors move and groove through the streets. No two bodies do it just the same, and this bold ballet is what makes the city sing. Shuffle and spread your deck just the same way: inhabiting its energies in your own special style. Maybe you'll want to flip through the pack quickly and tightly, keeping the cards close together as if you were beelining for a taxi on your way to a Midtown morning meeting. Or maybe you'll want to sprawl as you shuffle, taking the town by storm as you let all seventy-eight cards sweep across the floor.

Posing questions and creating spreads is a proprietary process that will build over time, just like an intimate relationship with an urban place. The more you talk to your deck, the more it'll talk back. Together, you'll find your secret spots, your singular shuffles, and your special spreads.

You can use the spreads below to begin....

THE NEW YORK SECOND SPREAD

This spread is made for the down-and-dirty moments when you need an intuitive hit on the fly. Arrive to your deck how-ever you like and pluck a single card, shaping a question that feels expansive and open-ended expressive, such as:

Pizza Slice: *What does this moment want to serve me, and how can I learn to snack on it?*

City Grid: *Where am I in my life right now, and how can I orient myself within this locale?*

Top-of-the-Rock: *What is the larger perspective being offered in this situation, and how can I pan out?*

Central Park: *What lives at the center of my life right now; what is the heart of this matter?*

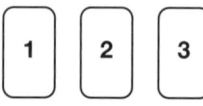

THE EMPIRE STATE OF LIFE SPREAD

This spread is perfect for understanding the multiple levels of a life moment. Separate your deck into three piles—Majors, Minors, and Court Cards—and select one from each pile:

Major Arcana: *The What*. This card gives you a sense of the big picture, the soul meaning of your situation.

Minor Arcana: *The How*. This card indicates the action you might adopt to help navigate it.

Court Card: *The Who*. This card awakens the part of your identity that's most needed as you walk through it.

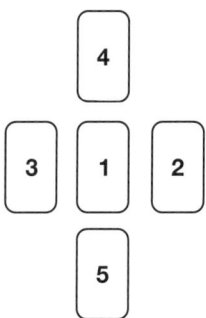

THE FIVE-BOROUGH SPREAD

If you're ready to dive a little deeper, you might inquire about a situation or current life moment and pick five cards from your pack:

Card 1: *Manhattan.* The larger-than-life, iconic borough of must-see sights, this card represents the whole shebang of your situation. Use it to commune with the must-know, matters-most in your current moment.

Card 2: *Brooklyn.* The brownstone borough of stoop-sitting neighborhood bustle, this card represents the fire in your situation. Use it to commune with the personal style and flair you might adopt as you move through this moment.

Card 3: *Queens.* The borough that gives rise to the city's airports, elevated train lines, and multitudinous languages, this card represents the air in your situation. Use it to commune with new attitudes and unstick yourself from whatever feels "same old."

Card 4: *The Bronx*. The only borough attached to solid land, and home to some of the city's most glorious residential architecture, this card represents the earth in your life moment. Use it to strengthen your sense of endurance, competence, and self-sufficiency.

Card 5: *Staten Island*. Surrounded by beaches and reached by the infamous orange ferry, this card represents the water in your situation. Use it to commune with the intuitive wisdom and subconscious emotional content that wants integrating in this moment.

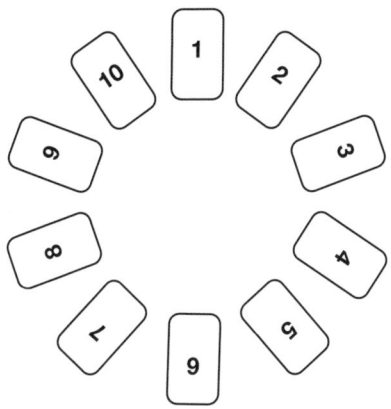

THE UNLIMITED METROCARD SPREAD

This spread is for those moments where you want the full, deluxe edition urban experience of life. Shuffle up your cards any way you see fit, and then pluck ten cards from the pack to represent the ten subway lines in the city, arranging them however you fancy. If you're in NYC, you might even spend the day riding the rails and pulling a card as you alight on each line.

Card 1: *The A/C/E.* The longest line in the system, stretching from the cliffs of Inwood all the way to the wave wilds of Rockaway, this card represents the exhale of expansion available in your situation. Tap its energies to embrace the adventure that's being offered up right now.

Card 2: *The B/D/F/M.* The only line to shimmy into four out of five boroughs, this card represents the greatest hits in your situation. Tap its energies to make the best out of whatever's on hand and stay more present for the ride.

Card 3: *The G.* The little train that could, busy bopping back and forth inside the borough of Brooklyn, this card represents the internal stability in your situation. Tap its energies to ground down into your inner resources and cultivate a sense of security.

Card 4: *The L.* Straight-shooting a horizontal line across Manhattan and Brooklyn, this card represents the clear through-thread in your situation. Tap its energies to part the clouds of confusion and see what matters most at the heart of it all.

Card 5: *The J/Z.* Flinging its fronds through parts of the city that some travelers don't usually tread, this card represents the secret treasures in your situation. Tap its energies to draw hidden ideas and emotions to the surface for integration.

Card 6: *The N/Q/R/W.* Seabeach-ing its way through the hometown hoods of Brooklyn and Queens, this card represents the roots of your situation. Tap its energies to discern the difference between nourishing habit patterns and comfort zones that are ready for renovation.

Card 7: *The 1/2/3.* From the birthplace of hip-hop in the Boogie Down Bronx and coursing the length of Broadway, this card represents the creative forces at play in your situation. Tap its energies to boost your confidence and connect with your natural talents.

Card 8: *The 4/5/6.* Powering rush-hour rides from Grand Central through Wall Street, this card represents the evolutionary work in your situation. Tap its energies to divine where a little down-and-dirty effort might be needed in the name of soul growth.

Card 9: *The 7.* Elevating its way through the multicultural mixology of Queens, this card represents the adaptability in your situation. Tap its energies to open up to increased possibilities and shifting perspectives.

Card 10: *The S.* Running shuttles along 42nd Street, Franklin Avenue, and Broad Channel to Rockaway, this card represents the immediate action in your situation. Tap its energies to inspire a next-step action that will help move you a little way down the line.

The
Major
Arcana ↘

The Major Arcana cards ask us to embrace the iconic energies of the Big Apple and learn to inhabit their emotional environments.

The Fool
JFK Arrival

Welcome to New York. Whether you're careening toward the city on your first flight into the fray with a cup of bubbly perched on your tray table, or are homeward-bound with apartment keys in hand, the Fool is here to remind you that here, absolutely anything can happen. The number on this tarot card is "0," which means that it functions outside the system of the other cards: a trapdoor that always exists, even beneath situations that seem the most solid. No matter where we find ourselves, this card asks us to liberate ourselves, just a little bit—releasing foregone conclusions and habitual grooves, and getting good with groundlessness, even for an instant.

Whenever we work with this card, we're invited to let the bottom fall out of some aspect of our lives. Maybe it's a relationship that's become suffocated by same-old roles. Or a work routine that's left us performing each action like an automaton. The Fool always arrives to throw the windows open wider and let the winds of mystery find us. On our journey through the seventy-eight cards of the tarot, it's in the Fool that we show up to life for the very first time. Can we be down for whatever's about to go down?

> *What is known in my life right now? What is unknown? And what is ultimately unknowable? How can I learn to love each of these three sensations more equally? What wants to come unstuck right now? How might I infuse a little more mystery into what I think I've got all figured out?*

CONCRETE JUNGLE: Explore the Fool's energy by engaging in acts of unsticking and aerating—wander off-grid and play with new routines. In NYC, embrace the fun-loving vertigo of riding one of the city's wildest subway routes: try taking the A train to Rockaway Beach and watch as the tracks seem to disappear as you skate across the surface of Jamaica Bay. Or, if you don't have time for a train trek, find exhilaration in the rush of air as you walk atop ventilation grates.

The Magician

Hailing a Cab

You're standing on the corner, poised for the arrival of *something*. This card might mean you're ready to green-light a project, a partnership, a new emotional way of being—channeling it right through you with antennae up and arm raised. The Magician marks the moment when we "hail" life: giving a little sign to signal that we're available for some on-duty magic to swoop us up from the sidewalk and send us on our way.

Whenever we work with this card, we're asked to explore our inspiration and creation process. No matter whether we're composing symphonies destined for Lincoln Center, or just fixing an artful plate of pasta in our studio apartment, each of us is a creatrix of possibility who intercepts life and translates it through us, leaving it forever flavored by our touch. With the Magician's help, we start to explore our style of leaving space for and awaiting hits of inspo:

seizing subtle possibilities in the moment and giving shape to the ethereal by bringing ideas into the material world.

What inspires me? How can I leave more space to allow inspiration to arrive? What is my creation process? How do I channel and bring things through myself? What is my relationship with moments of in-between-ness? How do I handle the gap before something arrives?

CONCRETE JUNGLE: Explore the Magician by wandering out into a landscape and seeing what catches your eye, then making something magical out of materials you have on hand. In NYC, alight on a park bench or stand on a street corner to catch overheard snippets of conversation, then integrate them into a poem. Listen to jazz ensembles riffing in the West Village or Harlem and then imagine playing alongside them, too. Notice the moment just before stoplights switch from red to green and ask yourself: Where will I go next?

The High Priestess

The Cloisters

Even beneath the hustle, the hush of the High Priestess always awaits us. Representing the vault of our inner wisdom, this card is the magnet that ushers us off life's main drags and into the potent place where we just know what we know, exactly when and how we know it. The High Priestess doesn't care about the hearsay overheard on the corner. This card doesn't heed the timed traffic lights or the crosswalk rush of the crowds. To find this sacred place, we often must travel against the tide, following what's timeless within us and letting it reach for us on its own time.

Whenever we work with this card, we're asked to await the answer to our question, however and whenever it arrives. And while we hang out, we can get curious about our inner dialogue with self. Sometimes we hear the word *intuition* and we think of instantaneous hits, sure things, and serene next steps. And sometimes the High Priestess delivers these kinds of answers. But rather than offering pat promises, this card wants us to learn how to listen. And to promise to listen to ourselves, no matter what.

> *What does silence sound like to me? What might a deeper dialogue with myself look like right now, and how could I support this kind of communion? When have I followed my intuition in the past, and where has it led me? When have I stifled my intuition, and where has that led me?*

CONCRETE JUNGLE: Explore the High Priestess by entering spaces that are designated for contemplation—anything from temples to quiet cars on moving trains. In NYC, notice transitions between cacophonous environments and hushed interiors: the respite of an air-conditioned lobby on a sweltering day, an unexpected greenspace arising amidst the steel, or the contemplative corner of a museum.

The Empress

Deli Decadence

If you're hungry, this city is for you: hawking skewers of spicy meats from street carts in 600-plus languages. Sandwich-boarding its extra specials from more than 20,000 restaurants. Spilling its to-go goodies from heaping shelves at all-night bodegas. When we meet the Empress, we're invited to partake of life's *more*-ness: siphoning sustenance out of the sensual experience of being alive.

When we work with this card, we're being asked to explore what it might mean to "have at" just a little bit more of life's bottomless brunch. It is a reminder that there is a form of nourishment in every moment, and that we have the right to partake of it. The Empress's arrival could be a reminder of the sweetness you've been resisting in a partnership because your palate has grown accustomed to obsessing over only the spicy or sour parts. Or it could be a call to pay attention to a situation that seems empty and hopeless, because there may be some secret snack still available within it that can serve your spirit. The deli of your life is open twenty-four hours, and while the grill may be closed at 3 a.m. there's always a frosted bun or a bag of chips that wants to power you up with pleasure until the next day.

Where does "fullness" exist in my life right now? What's my relationship to this more-ness, and what am I available to take in? What is the sensual inventory of my current situation: the tastes, sights, smells, and sounds that are on offer? What would just feel good?

CONCRETE JUNGLE: Explore the Empress through environments that are fertile and flooded with sensation, noticing what's fully saturated with color and scent. In NYC, revel in the olfactory plenty of the Brooklyn and Bronx botanical gardens; enjoy extra helpings from Indian buffets and dim sum carts; embrace the excess of the Dyker Heights Christmas lights display; and sidle up to the perfume counter at 5th Avenue department stores.

The Emperor
The Empire State Building

You have arrived. Feel the fierceness of your own footprint: the space you take and the iconic impact of your wake. The Empire State Building may no longer be the world's tallest, but the strength of its symbolic status is inarguable. Likewise, the Emperor's large-and-in-chargeness represents our right to be here. When we stand comfortably in its power, we become a behemoth without having to flex.

Whenever we work with this card, we're asked to explore our impact. Sometimes we'll pull it when we've been shy violet-ing into the pavement cracks, as a reminder that no matter how feeble we might feel, we still have the power to affect some facet of our own lives. Other times, we might flip it when our will has gone wild: here to assure us that we don't have to muscle to prove that we matter. Always a chance to check ourselves against these Goldilocks poles, the Emperor invites us to become "right-sized" in whatever our situation; it asks us to understand our special effects on the life that surrounds us, and to bear both the right and the responsibility to consciously wield the force that is us.

What would it mean to become "right-sized" in my current situation? Do I need to pump up my willpower, or tone it down just a little? When do I find myself flexing, and when do I play it small? What effect can I have in my life right now, and how can I take ownership of my impact?

CONCRETE JUNGLE: Explore the Emperor by noticing how things naturally take up space—watch trees spreading their roots or your own body entering a room. In NYC, play with shifting scales. Start with a visit to the Empire State Building, or another large-and-in-charge structure, and observe how city dwellers interact with this monolithic monument. Then spend some time in a small park or community garden. Notice how spaces of varying sizes make their impact felt and become important for the people who use them.

5

The Hierophant

The New York Public Library

A treasure trove of accumulated tales about the way it was—which inform the way it will be—the Hierophant wants us to become students of our own histories. And with the membership card to our own destinies firmly in hand, it asks us to survey the evidence gleaned from our experiences. When we know the full breadth of our accumulated knowledge, we can make informed choices about our actions.

This card is an invitation to unearth buried belief by considering our own muscle memories: all of the reactions, narratives, and behavior patterns we've stored, and how they continue to maintain their hold on us. The Hierophant wants us to explore these amassed materials—honestly assessing how they operate unconsciously, and whether they still serve our system. It also asks us to consider the internal resources we have access to: how we can dip into the living library that is our experience on this earth and let it nourish us in the here and now.

> *What are my strongest habit patterns? How did these arise, and which of these still serve me? Where is my current life situation "landing" within me—and what am I absorbing from it? What are my inherent resources right now—how could I draw upon what I already know and have?*

CONCRETE JUNGLE: Explore the Hierophant by investigating what you choose to hold, whether strong opinions or peach preserves in your pantry. In NYC, ground yourself in knowledge by exploring geology in Inwood Park, plumbing one of the subway's deepest stations at 63rd and Lex, or relishing the rich matter at DIA's Walter de Maria Earth Room. You could even sift through "visible storage" at one of the city's museums, or take the time to access generations of building records at City Hall's Municipal Library.

The Lovers
Washington Square Park

Immersed in the street symphony of one of the city's premier public squares, you become a locus of ephemeral exchange. Catching a stranger's gaze might set off dominos of delight that will last throughout the rest of their day. Sniffing a scent on the breeze could inspire you to search for the source. Life is always leading us elsewhere, and we are always leading it too. The Lovers card represents the realization that we are made from mutuality: multitudes of mini moments where we meet, greet, and move each other along.

Whenever we work with this card, we're asked to remember the reciprocity in our situation. Maybe we're embroiled in an actual love affair where our beloved seems to hold all the cards, and have forgotten that heart work is always a handoff. Or we're caught up in a project that doesn't seem to fit our grand plan, but may contain hidden wings that will carry us to our next way station. Wherever we find ourselves, the Lovers card invites us to become both the escort and the escorted: opening up to the unexpected roles that all parts of existence might play, ourselves included.

> *Where is the mutuality and reciprocity in my life right now? What types of exchanges and handoffs are happening? Who or what am I helping to guide, and who or what is helping to guide me? What am I longing for that seems "out there," and how might I boomerang it back?*

CONCRETE JUNGLE: Explore the Lovers by becoming aware of butterfly effects—imagining the unexpected ripples that one action might make. In NYC, immerse yourself in environments where multitudinous meet-and-greets are occurring: smoosh in with straphangers from Penn Station during rush hour, strut through vibrant shopping districts like Jackson Heights's Roosevelt Avenue or Fordham Road in the Bronx, or hit the dance floor at a club or in a ballet class.

7

The Chariot
Street-Food Cart

Every morning, before the sun rises, your favorite street-food cart sets off, full of everything necessary for the day. And you're just the same—leaving home for each day's explorations with your bundle strapped to your back. Just like these vital urban-hermit-crab packs, the Chariot is our reminder that we'll always be sheltered and stocked with necessary goodies, even as we move through life changes.

Whenever we work with this card, we're being asked to explore our maturation process and comfort zones. When we pull the Chariot, it could be time to rely on tried-and-true comfort foods to sustain us as we move toward a new beginning. Other times, we'll need to search for something more than a dirty water dog from our nearest corner cart—whether it's a rosé sipped while carriage-riding through Central Park, or pushcart shaved ice savored while biking through an unfamiliar borough. When the Chariot arrives, it's simply a message that we're being carried through a changing streetscape of some kind. And we can honor this shift however we wish. The Chariot reminds us that we can always ride in style—complete with whatever protection best umbrellas the beings we're becoming.

Where am I graduating from one level of life to another, and how can I best caretake myself through this maturation process? How do I cope with change? Which parts of my protective padding serve my growth right now, and which might want to be retrofitted?

CONCRETE JUNGLE: Explore the Chariot by watching how things get carried and delivered through change—whether it's an actual package, or a more metaphorical threshold-crossing. In NYC, come alive to all the shells and coverings that serve city life—like restaurant awnings, sidewalk sheds, horse-drawn carriages, and business suits worn as their owners race through the streets of Midtown—and see what physical armor you arm yourself with as you take to the streets.

8

Strength
Bodega Cat

From its pride of place perched beside the register, the mighty bodega cat beckons. Elsewhere in the city, the prospect of encountering animals might conjure frightful visions of rat attacks and pigeon swarms, but here inside the cozy corner store, you find yourself reaching out to feel for fur. In a city and a life that can sometimes seem cutthroat-cold, the Strength card asks us to show up and come forward in warm blood anyway—candidly confessing what's really in our hearts, and encouraging others to do the same by virtue of our own vulnerability.

Whenever we work with this card, we're asked to go first in some way, forgoing power plays in favor of the power of love. It might be an "I love you" or an "I'm sorry" said before we're assured of a guaranteed response. Or a chance to tenderize and share more, instead of feeling like we have to play it cool and keep our real feelings clutched to our chests. When we undo our clenched fists, drop our pretenses, and get a little bit more cuddly in this card's energy, we might be surprised by what snuggles up to meet our openhearted palm.

> *How can I "go first" in my life? What does vulnerability look like for me? Where might I be resisting revealing my true feelings, and why? How could I share more of my heart in this moment?*

CONCRETE JUNGLE: Explore Strength through situations that coax you forward and encourage earnestness: have a heart-to-heart with a friend, or play with children or pets. In NYC, see where you can let down your guard and choose candor: whether it's pulling out your headphones for a change and actually listening to the people around you, smiling at a stranger before you avert your gaze, or visiting a dog park or a cat café.

The Hermit
The High Line

High above the busy street, along a repurposed railway, the High Line offers a forested enclave of indigenous plant life. The Hermit's Highline represents the wooded spaces that await us when we're willing to walk within. While we may be among the millions, we are also always whole unto ourselves: self-regulating biospheres who invite patient inquiry and careful cultivation. In the Hermit card, we're invited to learn who we really are when we're wholly alone.

Whenever we work with this card, we're beckoned to go "solo" in some way. This could be a physical retreat from other humans and external demands. But we don't have to hermit ourselves too high above our everyday lives to experience its benefits. Harnessing its energy could be as simple as a lunch with yourself—just taking a moment to share a sandwich with the person you are. The Hermit only asks that we find a way back to ourselves, even in the crowd. We have the right to keep our own time, our pacing through life. And when we meet the people we actually are, where we are, we can decide exactly what's needed in this very moment.

> *What is my relationship to solitude? What would spending time truly "with" myself look like? What kind of person am I when I'm solo, and how does this differ from my public-facing self? How do I know when the time is right for something—how do I read the inner and outer signs?*

CONCRETE JUNGLE: Explore the Hermit through self-contained spaces: single rooms, bar stools, library carrels. In NYC, forgo the designated "must-sees" and design your own self-guided tour. And to achieve platinum Hermit status, engage in the ultimate city-insider act: tuck into a table for one near a restaurant window, where you can peep the multitudes securely from the safety of your own seat.

The Wheel of Fortune

The Wonder Wheel

Even within the city limits, there are carnival amusements for those who are brave enough to ride them. And when we slide into a seat and get whisked away, we can let the view from the top simply arrive—embracing our smallness in the face of a much larger destiny. Far beyond doomsday prophecies of good or bad fates, the Wheel of Fortune is here to remind us that life can surprise us all on its own.

Whenever we work with this card, we're asked to get curious about all the motions that are propelling us forward on our path. It invites us to welcome these adventurous chain reactions and accept that they don't always move in straight lines. Like the city that stays in perpetual motion, the Wheel wants to remind you to keep on turning without having to grasp the bigger picture just yet. When you stop trying to understand how life is going to get you from here

to there—wherever your "there" might be—you can kick back
and enjoy the ride.

*Where do I feel like I'm heading right now? Who or
what do I believe is controlling my course? How might
I show up for this moment more fully, without having
to understand where it's going to lead? If there were a
surprise package of life awaiting me, what would I want
to find inside?*

CONCRETE JUNGLE: Explore the Wheel of Fortune by
noticing how things "run" in your world, paying attention to
all the visible and invisible acts that lead you from point A
to B during a given day. In NYC, honor movement you don't
have to control by visiting the Transit Museum or sampling
multiple transportation modalities in a single day; place
your bets and take your chances at the Aqueduct racetrack;
or get spun right 'round on Jane's Carousel in DUMBO.

Justice
The Statue of Liberty

A beacon on the horizon, Liberty lifts its light beside the golden door. Like this keeper of the city's highest hopes and fiercest ideals, Justice asks us to interrogate how we can better uphold our own codes. This card illuminates the gap between our lives as they are and our lives as they might be. And in its daybreak, we're asked to honestly assess the choices we've made thus far, and whether choosing differently might fit us more fully as we move forward.

Whenever we work with this card, we're invited to examine what alignment actually feels like for us. We may find ourselves in the midst of a situation that everyone keeps telling us we're so lucky to have but that just feels "off" inside, no matter how hard we try to make it right. Or we'll realize we've been chasing an elusive ideal for years without even asking why, or whether, it actually matters to us. When Justice arrives, we're urged to forgo one-size-fits-all and instead do right by ourselves by answering to our own sense of right and wrong.

> *What is my personal code of conduct? How do I define what's right and wrong for me? When something feels "off," how do I sense this and how do I respond? What are my ideals, aspirations, and expectations, and do they still fit who I am? What's right for me, right now?*

CONCRETE JUNGLE: Explore Justice by reevaluating your own standards. Make a vision board, draft a new five-year plan, or take a personality test like the Myers-Briggs. In NYC, witness the fight for what's right at a City Hall public hearing; learn about the art of negotiation with a tour of the United Nations; or wander the streets of central Queens, Lower Manhattan, or the West Village, where buildings somehow find their right fit amidst piecemeal city planning.

12

The Hanged One

The Roosevelt Island Tram

Suspended in a cable car, city life seems to pause for a second. The traffic and people are still rushing far below, but from this sealed, soundless point, all the frantic ant-farm motions appear sweet and silly. Where is everyone going in their toy cars and on such tiny feet? The Hanged One is here to temporarily stop time in order for us to understand our current state more completely. In this place of hanging out without hurrying to move on, we start to realize that life isn't just about doing: sometimes it's about doing nothing, so that something can come undone.

Whenever we work with this card, we're invited to linger just a little while longer where we are and learn something more. Whether it's a life stage, project, or partnership that we feel we should be over and done with, we can sometimes feel "stuck" when we pull this card. Or, we might find ourselves clinging as something oh-so-slowly slips away. But the Hanged One doesn't want to leave us in limbo for no reason. Instead, it wants us to use our suspended state to look at this moment from new angles, and release into the process without having to push forward too quickly or hold on too long.

How are the timelines of my life unfolding, and how do I feel about these? How do I respond when I feel stuck? Which parts of my life want to be pushed forward, and which parts want to be left alone? How could I get more comfortable hanging out wherever I currently find myself?

CONCRETE JUNGLE: Explore the Hanged One through nearly invisible processes of unfolding, like watching a tiny plant grow each day. In NYC, play with remaining motionless while the city floods around you—coming to a standstill on a busy street corner and feeling the rush of life as it passes you by. Or enjoy some actual aerial suspension at the trapeze school on Chelsea Pier.

Death
The Sewage System

In the city that never sleeps, it can be hard to perceive the fade-outs and departures. Although NYC seems perpetually up and at 'em, it is still a part of nature. Rainwater rushes down a drain. A roach lies belly up like a scarab. And you are a part of it, too, shedding a little trail of your former self as you travel through these streets. In the dead of winter, you pack yourself into a puffy coat, and in the sweltering summer you let it all loose like a gushing fire hydrant. Rather than a doom-and-gloom harbinger of the ultimate end days, the Death card simply asks us to acknowledge what's always been true: that transformation is already an inherent part of us on a cellular level.

Whenever we work with this card, we're asked to acknowledge the season of change that is unfolding in our life, and to see how we might adopt a more natural posture within it. There might be a shift afoot. Or the call could be subtler: death may be a nod to notice the littlest leaves tinged with gold, a harbinger of more noticeable revolutions in the future. Whatever the morphing moment, Death asks us to honor both what is ephemeral and what is eternal. And while we may have strong notions about what's meant to stay and what's got to go, when we open to Death's dance, it just might surprise us. Yes, everything eventually ends. But in this town, the show must go on, too.

> *What is changing within me? What is changing around me? What would help me honor these transformations? And what do I know to be eternal and enduring? What season of life am I currently in: spring, summer, fall, winter? How can I meet myself there?*

CONCRETE JUNGLE: Explore Death through activities that match the current season—either within you or around you—like fall foliage tours or spring cleaning. In NYC, acknowledge the Universe's life/death cycles by witnessing late-night trash collection or visiting former-landfill-turned-park Freshkills. Discover biomorphic forms at the Noguchi Museum, or divine what's eternal while perusing the Met's Egyptian sarcophagi.

Temperance
Parade Balloons

From all the way down here on the ground, you look up and glimpse it: a billboard emblazoned with a message made just for you. A zeppelin-sized parade balloon amplifying itself to epic proportions. The larger-than-lifeness that lives in all of us, Temperance marks the moments when we open up to the bigness of being here. In its energy, we're encouraged to believe that our speck-like existence must have some kind of monumental meaning. Temperance asks us to co-create our story in conversation with the forces that exist beyond us.

Whenever we work with this card, we're invited to notice the signposts of our lives. Temperance can arrive when we feel like we've lost access to "what it all means" here to reassure us that our story is more than "just this." A continuation of the Wheel of Fortune's faith-building work, Temperance wants to remind us that our existence is always co-authored by spirit—a divine dialogue instead of a fixed fate. Whenever we give a name to what we're "all about," life can offer up even more of it. And soon, we start to see flashing neon signs of our soul purpose everywhere.

> *If I had to identify what my life has been "all about," what would I say? What are the themes that have repeated throughout my time on earth? What are my beliefs about the Universe at large? How do I connect to my own form of "god" or "spirit," however I understand it?*

CONCRETE JUNGLE: Explore Temperance through sudden feelings of fatedness, like noticing repeating signs during your day, or dialoguing with whatever your form of divinity. In NYC, look heavenward while standing under Grand Central's zodiac-inspired vaulted ceiling, celebrate spirit at the Chinatown New Year's parade or the Rockefeller Center Christmas tree lighting, visit a botánica, or pay homage at a local shrine like Our Lady of Mount Carmel Grotto in Staten Island.

The Devil
Times Square

This town runs on lust. At high noon or in the dead of night, the gritty glory of human desire is forever on decadent display. Whether it's technicolor emotions as a stranger bursts into tears on a street corner, or a ginormous billboard of covetable jewels coaxing you into excess expenditure, a bit of bestial beauty lurks on every corner. Here to make you look at and long for without turning away, the Devil strips us of stringent notions of sin and asks us to self-satiate with whatever gets us salivating.

Whenever we work with this card, we're urged to forgo good/bad assessments of our behavior, and start calling our own shots, shame-free. Often, the Devil will come through when we feel that an entity outside of ourselves seems to be pulling the strings. It could be another person, an institution, or even an inner part of us that's shaking the finger and chastising our choices. While we might enter this card's orbit feeling buttoned up into rigid roles and codes of conduct, the Devil always wants us naked cowboy-ing and spinning from the chandelier.

> *Where am I feeling the pressure of "shoulds"? Who or what is defining these standards of behavior? How do I exercise my own authority over my life? Where is it time to start calling the shots? Where am I ready to rebel, maybe even against my own standards for myself?*

CONCRETE JUNGLE: Explore the Devil by noticing your behind-closed-doors behaviors and experimenting with letting a little bit more of them out into the open. In NYC, experience the city after dark, even if it's just a trip to the 24/7 deli. Dare to cry or attract attention in public. Or channel the creative chaos of the city in the '70s with a crawl through East Village punk-rock haunts or the South Bronx, birthplace of hip-hop; or disco roller-skate at one of the city's revival rinks.

The Tower
The Parachute Jump

While the Parachute Jump ride may now be officially defunct, its ongoing function as a fluorescent boardwalk beacon and backdrop for celebratory fireworks is proof of a city whose charge can't be stopped. Likewise, despite its reputation for large-scale destruction, the Tower card wants to keep us lit and moving toward more life, waking us up to the sheer vitality that exists in each mojo-rich moment.

Whenever we work with this card, we're asked to come alive to all the forces at play in our situation, and to embrace the notion that we don't always have to be in charge of them. Often, the Tower comes calling when we feel like something's been unleashed that's beyond our conscious control. But this card never makes its moves out of malice. Instead, it's just a reminder of life's inherent heat. Sometimes we'll make strategic moves that'll power us toward the next place. And other times we'll get moved. We have the right to exercise our free will, and so does everything else.

> *What are all the forces unfolding in my life right now? Which of these do I feel like I'm consciously contributing to, and which feel like they're outside my conscious control? Where am I being asked to release the need to understand what's happening, and just "let live"?*

CONCRETE JUNGLE: Explore the Tower by feeling into the strong forces that are present in your life: whether it's letting yourself burst forth with a big emotion, or noticing energy that's generated during a frictional moment. In NYC, observe how bodies in motion negotiate the shared sidewalk; come alive to the aural combat of diverse street sounds competing for primacy; or witness the creative destruction present at a building-construction site or adaptive reuse of a historical structure.

The Star
Plaza Suite

City living has worn you down. You're burdened with shopping bags. You've spread yourself thin across the five boroughs. And now you're ready to return to center: the Star is the hotel suite where we repair and reunite our pieces, taking the time to better understand where we began.

Whenever we work with this card, we're invited to restore ourselves by tracing some element of our lives back to its source. This could signal a time of healing, where we exfoliate the calluses of accumulated hurts and recover the softer parts beneath that are asking for attention. It could also be a chance to understand the origin points within us, traveling to the source of a problem or a pattern that's been permeating our lives to see how it started. Or it could be a simpler kind of recharge, as we take a moment in a busy day to plug into something that renews our spirit, reviving a past passion and reigniting our resilience. Wherever it finds us, the Star wants to soothe the fractures and bring us back together again.

> *When I'm in need of a recharge, what are my sources of renewal? What wants to be traced back to its origins right now? Where am I ready to return to some earlier, more essential version of things? What parts of my life have been separated that are asking to be reunited?*

CONCRETE JUNGLE: Explore the Star through restorative experiences as literal as a trip to the spa or more conceptual: visit the site of an archaeological dig or your own birthplace. In NYC, embrace your original form with a sojourn at a Russian bathhouse or Koreatown spa, a polar bear plunge at Brighton Beach, or a power nap in your hotel room or apartment. You can also trace the city's indigenous origins at the National Museum of the American Indian.

The Moon
The Mermaid Parade

You're all the way out at the end of the line, immersed in Coney Island chaos: triple-fried clams, swords swallowed whole, and every shape of beautiful human body bared. You may have no idea how you got here. Maybe you missed your stop while fast asleep and somehow ended up dipped in glitter and emptied into the Atlantic. In the midst of this party, you may as well be on the Moon—but the secret is that the only way out is to wade even deeper.

Whenever we work with the Moon, it invites us into the woozy waves within us. Each of us contains a bit of paranormal activity, and when we pull the Moon, we're asked to stage a séance of self and allow some of our inner strangeness to "possess" us. It might be an inexplicable urge that has us sleepwalking toward an irrational choice at 2 a.m. Or an overwhelming emotion that rises to tidal proportions, even though it was inspired by something seemingly small.

A pull from a past life or an echo from this one that bends linear time.

How do I respond to overwhelming emotions and feelings that seem bigger than me? How do I navigate strong memories and pulls from the past? What inexplicable urges live within me right now? What wants to "take" me, and how could I let myself get taken?

CONCRETE JUNGLE: Explore the Moon by conjuring the irrational: go ghost-hunting, party till dawn, or just try walking a familiar path blindfolded to recognize its inherent strangeness. In NYC, commune with the faithful departed at the haunted Dakota building, visit the graves at the Marble Cemetery, or awaken the raven at the Edgar Allan Poe Cottage in the Bronx. And for a more personal experience of "the beyond," delight in disorientation by missing your subway stop, or loosening up at a Bushwick loft party or immersive theater experience.

The Sun
Central Park

Some of the city's tourist locales seem so blatantly obvious that they make "real" New Yorkers balk. Yet, while searching out the city's insider secrets can be satisfying, its what-you-see-is-what-you-get-ness is also part of its charm. And when you embrace the just-is-ness of something as simple as a saunter through this most iconic of parks, you find that this town can actually inspire trust in life. A break in the clouds of complexity, the Sun invites us to step straight into its honest truths without second-guessing.

Whenever we work with this card, we're being asked to get realer: to drop the fancy explanations in favor of simpler solutions and be as authentic as possible. Maybe this card is highlighting a relationship where you endlessly over-analyze and have forgotten how to actually *be* with your partner. Or it brings to mind a comment that you've anxiously spun into a huge problem instead of recognizing that it was meant exactly as it was said. The Sun can also reveal where we may be justifying instead of just calling it: making excuses for behavior, or lingering in the layers that keep us from living life as it is.

What is showing up in my life right now, and how can I show up more authentically for it? What has become overly complicated, and how could I adopt a simpler approach or explanation? If I could reduce my situation to just a few words or thesis statements, what would they be?

CONCRETE JUNGLE: Explore the Sun through primary-colored sensations like birthday celebrations, inspirational quotes, and freshly laundered sheets. In NYC, whether you're a visitor or a resident, find joy in classic tourist experiences like a Rockefeller Center ice-skating trip, a carriage ride in Central Park, catching a Broadway show, or dinner at a Little Italy red-sauce joint. Strip down at the Rockaways' nude beach, or engage in some real talk with your cabdriver.

Judgment
Manhattanhenge

You're standing on a street corner, and suddenly the forces align: the sun's tilt matches the city's grid and the concrete canyons flood you with light. Awake to the entirety, you sense that your little life is also part of something more huge and holy. Like a eulogy that happens while we're still alive, Judgment offers each one of us its mighty mercy. It asks us to find forgiveness for all our human efforts, and to summon the courage to collaborate with our own continued evolution.

When we work with this card, its monolithic meaning might seem hard to access on an everyday basis. And this is for good reason, as this archetype wants us to "scale up"— opening to the larger forces of nature that power through us. Like the Tower's fiery force, Judgment asks us to make love to the magnetics of life. This might mean reckoning with a pattern of behavior or form of partnership that's already pushing its way out of our lives—we might keep going through the motions for a while, but it just won't feel the same. Or it could mean making peace with a part of our lives that we won't ever be able to "fix" fully. By giving up the fight, we might actually give ourselves the grace to go onward. Rather than rendering us weak, when we find forgiveness for the natural fault lines of our lives—accepting what might never shift, and rising to meet what absolutely must move—we grow even larger. At peace with the entirety of our lives, we're now ready to evolve into our most powerful form yet.

What things may never change in my lifetime, what inevitable changes are already underway, and how can I handle both of these? Where am I being asked to find forgiveness, either for myself or for forces outside of me? What is my definition of power? Where can I find more peace?

CONCRETE JUNGLE: Explore Judgment through sites of epic wonder and natural potency like national parks, wind farms, and energy vortexes. In NYC, commune with the colossus of the cosmos at the Hayden Planetarium; move with the masses at a Yankees, Mets, or Cyclones baseball game; enjoy operatic glory at Lincoln Center; play with power by visiting the New York Stock Exchange; or find forgiveness at St. John the Divine's Peace Fountain.

The World
The Unisphere

Constructed for the epic 1964 World's Fair that would usher the city into the space age, the Unisphere remains the world's largest globe and holds court from the borough of Queens—one of the most multicultural urban areas on the planet. At the end of our Major Arcana journey from 0 to 21, the World card holds it all; it asks us to receive the wisdom of our experiences, work within our limitations, and assess the legacy we're leaving behind.

Whenever we work with this card, we're invited to weigh our lives in some way: facing up to finiteness and deciding what really matters. Sometimes, the World arrives when it's time for closure. Whether it's the be-all and end-all of a job, relationship, or way of being in the world, this card can invite us to honor life's grand finales. And at other times it might invite us to commune with the curtain call that's going to come for us all, at the very end. But rather than a grim trip straight to the grave, we can use this card's gravity to find meaning: evaluating what we're willing to put our weight behind for the long haul, and figuring out where exactly to send our precious fuel while we're still here.

> *Where is something in my life culminating, and how can I celebrate this? How do I handle endings, the limits of time, and my own human limitations? What matters most to me, and how can I put more of my weight behind it? What kind of legacy do I want to leave behind?*

CONCRETE JUNGLE: Explore the World through environments that build endurance and honor endings, like finish lines, commitment ceremonies, and movie montages. In NYC, take a tour through all the spaces that have held meaning for you during your time here; touch down in all five boroughs during a single day; cheer participants through the paces of the New York City Marathon; and have a look at the whole city in miniature at the Queens Museum Panorama.

The Minor Arcana ↘

The Minor Arcana are street symphonies: the bump-and-grind of living and learning at ground level, they ask us to apply their magic in immediate, tangible, and practical ways.

THE WANDS
Fire Escapes

This is the suit where we learn to ignite our fundamental life force, express our individual essence, inject our lives with larger-than-life meaning, and regulate our energy expenditure—from the spark of a lighter on a park bench to a full-on Fourth-of-July fireworks display.

The Ace of Wands

→ *In this city, there are signs of life everywhere, from the people pounding the pavement, all the way down to the tiniest blades of grass pushing up through the sidewalk cracks.*

Each Ace in the tarot is our initiation into its element. It asks us to notice where the element's powers are already present in our lives, and to then send increased attention in that direction. Here in the fire of the Wands suit, we're invited to view our lives as a heat map: the Ace of Wands means taking an inventory of where the warmth of our passions exists so that we can turn toward what fires us up and away from what's no longer turning us on. Whenever we work with this card, we're asked to come at our lives leaner and cleaner, without excessive drama or unnecessary analysis. When we respond to its on/off, yes/no questions, we start stoking the sparklers that actually want to get lit.

> *Which parts of my life are switched "on" right now, which are switched "off," and how can I respond accordingly?*

STREET SIGNS: Look for "signs of life" and explore how things get turned on for the first time—whether it's slipping your key into the car ignition, or watching your pup race out into the back yard. In NYC, take a moment at dusk to notice the tiny lights being switched on in apartment windows as the sun goes down.

The 2 of Wands

→ *You swing through the revolving doors and hit the pavement at full speed. Strutting through the streets, you leave your indelible mark on everything you touch.*

Each of the tarot's 2s contains the essence of the Major Arcana's number 2 card, the High Priestess, in its DNA. These cards ask us to listen in for our own wisdom, and practice using the element's properties in our own style. Here in the 2 of Wands, we're urged to come out of the cocoon with a rallying cry, engaging with life in a playful way like a baby learning its own strength for the very first time. Whenever we work with this card, we're asked to enjoy our own capacity for action: it asks us to do something, *anything*, to remind ourselves that we're here, alive, and capable of making whatever it is happen.

> *What one move could I make right now, however*
> *seemingly small, to remind myself that I am the*
> *protagonist of my own life?*

STREET SIGNS: Explore this card by taking action that distinguishes you as an individual: notice how it feels when you raise your hand to answer a question or pen your name to a project. In NYC, become aware of your own body forging a path through a crowd, or watch as basketball players make magic moves at the West 4th Street courts.

The 3 of Wands

→ *Everyone seems to be honing their hustle—hell-bent on getting better, bolder, faster. Yet at the heart of this endless quest for improvement lies the ultimate dare: to start from scratch as each day breaks.*

Each tarot 3 is descended from the Major Arcana's Empress card, and is an invite to welcome more of life's bold beauty. Ruled by the element of fire, the 3 of Wands wants us to actually relish our right to accept challenges—spreading our mojo around without worrying about our technique. This card urges us to connect with the relentlessness of our spirit. Whenever we work with it, we're asked to summon the courage to try again and start over and over, losing track of the straight lines of progress and instead letting ourselves live and learn as we go.

What challenge would I take on if I knew I wouldn't be evaluated through a success/failure paradigm?

STREET SIGNS: Tap the joy that can be found in both DIY hobbies and mastery—like singing in the shower, and then listening to a famous opera. In NYC, find arenas where novices can function alongside virtuosos: bust a move to street music, regardless of how much rhythm you've got; or join a chess, dominos, or bocce game in a public park, no matter what your skill level.

The 4 of Wands

→ *For a moment, the city seems to run on glorious fumes without having to work so damn hard. Trains, traffic, and people flow forward, fueled by the friction that's already been generated.*

Each of the tarot's 4s is a baby of the big Major Arcana 4, the Emperor. We can use these cards to land within each of their respective suit's elements and embrace stability. In the Wands' fire suit, this is our opportunity to actually receive the heat that's already been created through our efforts. This could mean a pause from endless output to celebrate a mini-win along the way. Or it could mean giving yourself permission to just coast for a little while, carried by the momentum that's already built from your striving. In a suit that's so often about doing, this card wants us to trust that we've already done more than enough.

> *How do I know when I've done "enough," and how can I celebrate the efforts I've already made?*

STREET SIGNS: Connect with a passion that doesn't feel like hard work, and notice how pleasurable it feels to receive and get powered up by your love for it. In NYC, get toasty beside a "hot nuts" cart, or eat what you've cooked at a Japanese BBQ or park grill pit.

The 5 of Wands

➔ *All day long, this town is throwing tantrums. Conflagrations
and gesticulations. Bodies burning off steam with a push and
a shove. Through constant catharsis, the city still stands.*

Each of the tarot's 5s turns up the spice on life. Like the
Major Arcana's 5 card, the Hierophant, they draw what's
stored within us to the surface. And then they ask us to
gain more mastery over our matter. In the 5 of Wands, the
heat is on, and we may find ourselves pitching some flavor of tantrum as we "have it out" with some part of our
lives. But rather than tamping down this embattled energy,
this card actually calls us to forge a greater loyalty with ourselves through whatever the fight. By abiding our angst, we
become a ride-or-die real friend to self, sticking by our own
side through the friction.

*Where do I want to just "have it out" right now, and how
can I support my own catharsis?*

STREET SIGNS: Let yourself get sweaty and physical in
this energy, running in place, yelping, or shaking your body
out. In NYC, race up a set of stairs or engage in parkour if
you're feeling extra fit; yell as the noise of an oncoming train
approaches; or fight against a fierce wind tunnel.

The 6 of Wands

→ *You are feeling yourself, from foot to crown. You catch*
a glimpse of your glory in a passing windowpane, and
power up with a personal soundtrack that carries you just
above the crowd.

Each of the tarot's 6s marks our return to life's sweetness
after the catharsis of the 5s. Kindred spirits with the Major
Arcana's Lovers, these cards invite us to come into deeper
communion with the energies of reciprocity and exchange.
In the Wands' fire element, we're asked to let ourselves be
beheld: seen in our essential dignity with fame-worthy flag
flying. This could mean learning to accept some adoration.
Or it could manifest as a moment of beholding your own
beauty. Maybe you could even enhance the epic quality of
your life with some healthy drama—celebrating your one-
life-to-live by amplifying your most passionate feelings.
In the 6 of Wands, we are meant to see and be seen, our
names written in larger-than-life lights.

> *What parts of me need to feel more seen right now, and*
> *what aspect of my life wants to become "larger-than"?*

STREET SIGNS: Pump up some element of your life,
whether it's teased hair or a dramatic entrance. In NYC, take
a tour of famous movie and television filming locations, and

delight in the collision between these everyday environments and their more epic imagined scale.

The 7 of Wands

→ *When you look more closely at each human who passes, you notice that not one of these beings is exactly the same as any other. Each strutting city dweller cuts their own singular shape.*

Each of the tarot's 7s is descended from the Major Arcana's Chariot—here to help us challenge our comfort zones and competently care for ourselves. In the Wands' fire-branded 7, we're asked to embrace doing our own thing without worrying about how anyone else is doing it. So often, we fear we're about to be replaced by a better version of us and scramble to secure evidence of our continued relevance. But this 7 wants to remind us that we're irreplaceable by the grace of just being. When we lean on this card, we no longer have to protect our personal flair, because there's no one else who will ever be able to "do us" quite like we can.

≡ *What inner qualities do I possess that no one else could ever duplicate?*

STREET SIGNS: Spend time doing your "thing"—becoming totally absorbed in an activity or way of being that you're an easeful expert in. In NYC, notice personal flair on passersby; taste multiple takes on a classic New York dish; or read each name on Ellis Island's Wall of Honor.

The 8 of Wands

→ *The streets are already in full swing—a sped-up celebration of scents, sounds, and sights. Choose your own adventure and follow the signs that give you the high sign.*

Like their forebear, the Major Arcana's Strength card, all tarot 8s want us to snuggle closer to them and release our resistance. In the Wands' bonfires, it's time to loosen up and let it rip as we let life fling itself at us like a piñata party and see what we can catch in our upturned palms. Whenever we work with this card, we're asked to read the signs of our lives like a scavenger hunt—noticing the little synchronicities and symbols from Spirit that keep repeating, and actually following them on an adventure. And we're asked to DIY whatever's arriving: not only making do with what we "get," but also making more magic out of it.

≡ *What are the signs of my life telling me right now? And how can I make something out of these symbols?*

STREET SIGNS: Take a day to treat your entire life like a tarot deck, interpreting signs and symbols in your environment. In NYC, stage a scavenger hunt; or revel in some DIY action with an off-off-Broadway show, or an outfit fashioned from pieces picked up while thrifting.

The 9 of Wands

➔ *You're on the verge of melting into the pavement or collapsing onto a bench, loaded with the packages of go-hard living. Take a New York second. You're in this for the long haul, after all.*

The tarot's 9s are descended from the Major Arcana's Hermit card, and each of them calls us to a solitary experience of their element. In the go-hard-or-go-home Wands suit, it's time for a time-out. It could be the tiniest touch-in with yourself for a few minutes in the bathroom, as you splash some water on your face and catch a glimpse of the glint in your eyes that'll help you go forward. Or it could be a more dramatic decompression where you step out of the game for days. The tarot's form of interval training, the 9 of Wands is our locker-room pit stop with self, where we summon our inner cheerleader and get ourselves together for round two.

≣ *How do I manage my energy levels, and what does self-sustainability look like for me?*

STREET SIGNS: Imagine that you're your own coach, and give yourself the halftime encouragement and assistance you need to carry on. In NYC, take a lunch break with workers in Lower Manhattan or Midtown, or enjoy intermission at a Madison Square Garden sporting event.

The 10 of Wands

➜ *While the city glistens with golden opportunities, there's only so much you can do, see, and eat in a single day. As the sun sets over the Hudson, you settle your scores and reset your sights.*

The tarot's 10s are infused with Wheel of Fortune card essence. Each marks a culmination of our journey through its suit, and asks us to release some of our control and make peace with our path thus far. In the Wands' fiery heat, we start a conversation between the human us and the heroic us. This might mean assessing our definitions of winning and losing, and adjusting our standards of success. Or it could mean giving up a war we've been waging our whole lives that's just not ours to fight. This card reminds us that living within our limitations can be a courageous act, as we build more of our personal power by embracing what we're actually meant to handle.

> *What kind of hero am I? Which battles are mine to fight, and which struggles are ready to be released?*

STREET SIGNS: Identify your top three superpowers and commit to a day where you only take on missions that match them. In NYC, hone your focused strength while observing tai chi in Chinatown, playing handball, or joining a demonstration in Union Square.

THE CUPS
To-Go Cups

This is the suit where we compassionately care for our many selves, understand the primal patterns within our lives, regenerate our hearts, and allow for emotional release— from an air-conditioner droplet to the salty sea that surrounds this city of islands.

The Ace of Cups

→ *The first raindrops to pavement summon a soft scent up from the street. The rush of cars and people through falling water hushes the hustle and you tuck inside.*

The tarot's Aces welcome us into primary presence with their element, giving us a glimpse of its magic properties for the very first time. Here, in the Cups' element of water, we sniff rain in the air, turn a bathtub tap on, or take a little sip from our glass. There is nothing we have to "do" in this card except notice the physical and symbolic role water occupies right now. Maybe we're parched and thirsty for its cleansing and cooling—desiccated from too much strenuous effort and heady emotional processing. Or maybe we're absolutely flooded with feeling, so inundated with tears that it's time for a towel-off. Wherever we are, this card helps us care for the flow.

> *What taps of emotion want to be turned on within me? Which are already flowing freely, and how can I tend them?*

STREET SIGNS: Explore your relationship to water, noticing your preferences for different experiences of it within and on your body, from a cup of tea to an ocean skinny-dip. In NYC, travel from wherever you are to the water's edge, and remember that you are inhabiting an archipelago.

The 2 of Cups

→ *We grow up fast in the city, often tamping down tenderness in favor of toughness. But this town can always hold more of us, if we're willing to hold our many selves closer.*

Each of the tarot's 2s brings us face-to-face with ourselves as seen through the eyes of that element. Here, in the watery 2, it's a chance to soften the edges of our self-gaze and extend a loving touch to the parts of us we may have roughed up. This might mean integrating a part of ourselves that we constantly push away and deem not worthy of compassion. Or it could mean standing strong and silencing a voice that wants to tear us down from the inside out, without adding extra layers of self-recrimination for its existence in the first place. A homecoming for all our tender teenage pieces, the 2 of Cups wants us to invite each of them to dance.

> *Which pushed-away parts of me are being asked to come closer? Which parts have strong-armed their way inside that might not have a place any longer?*

STREET SIGNS: Jot down some of the parts of you that arise during the day, and give them neutral nicknames, just noticing who they are and what they want. In NYC, travel to Central Park's boathouse and offer your reflection a softer gaze as you row through the still waters.

The 3 of Cups

→ *Trios of friends sharing their souls while dining al fresco. A spontaneous confession from a stranger. This city harbors as many shapes of the human heart as there are lovers alive.*

Each of the tarot's 3s is a proliferation of the element's forms; it shows us that there is more than just a two-way, either/or path through its teachings. In the heart-centric work of the Cups suit, this 3 is our primer in practical intimacy. Sometimes it arrives when we're holding fast to a notion about where we should be on our emotional journey, or what our relationships should look like. Instead, this card wants us to inquire about the current state of our heart as it is, and to let others offer us the same honesty without getting defensive. No longer caught up on protecting a perfected form of aspirational loving, we learn what real love really looks like for us.

How can I invite more honesty into my relationship with myself and others; and what can the present state of my heart teach me about real love?

STREET SIGNS: Create closeness by accepting emotional feedback without critique, and asking and answering "How are you?" honestly. In NYC, build intimacy with the city by kicking back at a local haunt in a non-touristy neighborhood where people are just living their lives.

The 4 of Cups

→ *Sample cups on the sidewalk being shoved into your hands. Solicitous stares begging you to share. Sometimes, this city's emotional exposure can be too much for a heart to handle.*

The tarot's 4s are our check-in-ready suites of self-stabilization. Here, in the watery 4, we're invited to take some time out to sift through the emotional experiences we've been through, and to figure out under what conditions, and with whom, we actually feel safe to share our hearts. Working with this card asks us to honor our own process of becoming available, regardless of others' timelines or expectations about our readiness to come forward, or our own fears about missing out on moments of intimacy. By waiting until our emo waves stabilize, we can then offer ourselves up from a space of soul-secure serenity.

What does emotional safety look like for me, and what does my heart need time off from?

STREET SIGNS: Create a list of trusted confidants and environmental supports that bolster your ability to feel emotionally secure. In NYC, nestle into a nautical heart haven at Snug Harbor on Staten Island, or clear your emotional waters in Roosevelt Island's Four Freedoms Park.

The 5 of Cups

➜ *You stand before the building, searching beneath the brick. Something else once stood here, but you can't remember what. In this city, the hauntings hit you through the tiniest holes.*

The 5s of the tarot are our soul workouts—here to train our muscles into mastery through some exploratory angst. In this watery 5, we begin to probe the notion of emotional absence. When we work with this card, it doesn't have to signal all-out grief for a major loss, but it does want us to dance with whatever's no longer here. This could mean honoring a version of yourself who once was, or the poignant end of a project. Or even just the little bits of uncompleted intentions that fall away at the end of the day. Wherever the sweetheart holes exist, the 5 of Cups wants us to bring our presence to the emptiness that's left behind.

What's gone from my life, and how can I honor the space that it's left behind?

STREET SIGNS: Stage a going-away ceremony for whatever is no longer present—whether it's a person, place, or way of being. In NYC, notice graffiti tags and "I was here" markers of former presence; suss out multiple layers of history on a sign; or stand before an empty lot.

The 6 of Cups

→ *You've been holed up all winter with the radiators clanging. And one day, just like that, the ice melts. You step outside your door into springtime. Here you are again. It's been you, all along.*

The 6s of the tarot ladle us back into life's punch bowl—inviting our spirits to participate anew after the necessary isolation of the 5s. Like a comeback ballad, the 6 of Cups wants us to love life once again, despite all the livings and losings we've been through. This card offers us emotional renewal and regeneration, and also reminds us of the sweet, core self who's been at the heart of our story all along. No matter how many times we've been through whatever our version of "it" is, the 6 of Cups is the soft-feathered phoenix who teaches us resilience through heart-openness—reminding us that we've still got more than enough good loving to give.

How do I handle the seasons of my heart, and stage comebacks after losses? And what have I always loved, through it all?

STREET SIGNS: Chart the story of your heart over time, outlining its valleys of loss and peaks of open loving, and bearing witness to your survival through it all. In NYC, celebrate springtime comebacks with a trip to Chelsea's flower district, or belt out a ballad at a karaoke bar.

The 7 of Cups

→ *A lusty look into a shop window. An afternoon craving that sends you through the streets tracking down a singular flavor. Whatever your obsession, hunt it through the concrete jungle.*

The tarot's 7s all invite us to interrogate externally imposed expectations. In the emotional Cups suit, we're asked to follow our urges, wherever they may lead. This card can come calling when we feel like we've got to decide what's "best" for us, as a reminder that we're allowed to sample a range of sensations without knowing exactly how they'll serve. It can also arise when we fear we've gotten overly preoccupied with a particular passion, here to help us let ourselves get a little bit obsessed and consumed. A companion into our carnal depths, the 7 of Cups just wants us to want whatever we're wanting.

What are my current obsessions? Beyond good versus bad desires, what do I want right now?

STREET SIGNS: Let yourself get totally absorbed into a desire, spending all day learning about or experiencing your chosen passion. In NYC, follow a delicious scent or a faraway sight to its source, or scratch your primal itch by reading about human exploits on Page Six.

The 8 of Cups

➜ *You slip away. Down an alley. Into a crowd. Anonymous for a moment. Losing the hard edges of yourself and telling no one of your whereabouts, you disappear to reappear, reformed.*

The 8s of the tarot massage the places in us that have grown taut, and tenderize us toward more options. In the feeling-based Cups suit, this 8 is our emotional elopement. It's a chance to engage in a little bit of good ghosting from life, disappearing out the back door of a pattern, project, or relationship. This could mean turning away from something that seems good on paper but isn't fulfilling a deeper soul calling. Or remaining physically present in a situation, but retreating energetically. This slippery 8 wants us to learn to love ourselves through loosening, going walkabout to relocate who and where we really are in our own hearts.

What am I being called to fade out from right now, and how can I slip away?

STREET SIGNS: Notice all the moments of loosening in your life, whether it's parting ways with a friend, watching the sun sink, or undoing your shoelaces. In NYC, duck into an arthouse film matinee or watch Manhattan receding while riding the Staten Island ferry.

The 9 of Cups

→ *Whether you're a native or a newbie, you've got a New York
dream glittered across your heart. Whatever you do and
wherever you go, find a way to keep it alive.*

Each tarot 9 asks us to nurture the nuance that is us. In the
watery Cups suit, this 9 is made from fantasy foam, and it
asks us to hope and believe that the best is yet to come.
It may also beckon us to believe the best in ourselves and
others and wish more wondrousness out of what is—helping
each other rise to the fairy-tale occasion. In the face of life's
sticky bits and reality reckonings, the call of this card can
feel like a radical act. We might find ourselves questioning
whether we're delusional, or if we deserve whatever we're
imagining. But the treasure of the 9 of Cups is already ours
whenever we allow ourselves to join our own dream team.

*Even if it feels like the stuff of pure fantasy, what am I
most hoping will happen?*

STREET SIGNS: Make like a little kid and wish upon a star,
a fountain coin, or a dandelion. In NYC, ascend Belvedere
Castle; visit the Unicorn tapestries; try on fancy threads at a
department store; or gaze longingly at an apartment building you'd love to inhabit.

The 10 of Cups

➜ *Nothing here stays the same for more than a few seconds. The traffic lights turn over. Your cells change. In the face of all that's fleeting and flashing, be here for it now.*

The 10s are our celebration ceremony of their suit, where we party on alongside all we've lived and learned. In the touchy-feely Cups, we've walked through every shade of the human heart, and now we're ready to release completely and trust that we can sail through each passing sensation with ulti-mate sensitivity. A reminder of the eventual evanescence of every human experience, this card teaches us the fine art of being "here for it" while it's still here. Wherever you are, the 10 of Cups wants you to be there completely—relishing whatever goodness can be found from the present moment before it's as good as gone.

When I remember that this moment won't last, what sweetness can I find within it?

STREET SIGNS: Immerse yourself in this magic moment by naming five joyous things you notice in your environment right now. In NYC, stay present until the end with a dawn-to-dusk beach day or sunset river cruise; or people-watch at a café, content and complete exactly where you are.

THE SWORDS
The Subway System

This is the suit where we observe the swirl of our consciousness, create space in our nervous systems, separate the truthiest truths from the stuck stories, and ride out beyond imagined limits—from the little G train that could, to the A's farthest Rockaway reaches.

The Ace of Swords

➜ *The just-before-daybreak stillness as the subway stations await the rush. For a few magical moments, the system seems almost empty. Poised for love at the very first swipe.*

The Aces are "of" their element, pure and simple, and ask us to turn to face them with an open spirit. In the Swords suit, we stand before the blank page and strip ourselves of expectation. Like a flutter of wind from the Fool's full-on existentialism, this card asks us to embrace more of life's what-ifs. This could mean a pause where you let someone answer before you rush to respond. Or attending to a pinprick of possibility and watching it grow into a portal. Or cultivating willingness to ask a question and handle the reverb of whatever the reveal. Our spirit's handheld fan, this Ace wants us to bring on the breeze of a beginner's mind.

> *Where can I release expectation and open to possibility instead?*

STREET SIGNS: Notice how many times you "fill in a blank," whether it's someone else's sentence or an imagined outcome, and leave some space instead. In NYC, watch streets and subway platforms getting swept and power-washed during the wee hours.

The 2 of Swords

→ *Competing buskers, the assault of announcements, the shove of strangers. To survive the system, you've got to drop down into the soundless place inside while you ride.*

The tarot's 2s are our intuitive channels—here to hold us steady in a container of our own wisdom. Amidst the swirl of the Swords' possibilities, this card wants us to find the still point inside ourselves before we rush to others' conclusions. It often comes calling when we've gotten hung up on life's feedback loops: chasing external approvals, dragged into someone else's drama, or fearing the fallout from a choice we've made. Channeling its powers means building a pop-up tent of spacious self-protection around us at a moment's notice. Inside our portable consciousness chambers, the only counsel we seek is our own.

≡ *What feedback am I soliciting right now, and why?*

STREET SIGNS: Practice making a decision or taking a small step toward something with absolutely no outside input, not even commentary from your own consciousness. In NYC, block out the overstimulating din with noise-canceling headphones or dark shades.

The 3 of Swords

→ *You calculate your approach. The timing of the arriving car, all other things being equal. But the trip must also be made in wild human style. Both sides of the platform want to ride.*

The tarot's 3s fan us open to a full-color version of life, filled with all shades of sensation. Through the perceptual lens of the Swords suit, this 3 teaches us to caretake our consciousness. Tending our thought patterns starts by assessing our head and our heart monitors and adjusting accordingly. Sometimes we'll be caught in a maudlin moment, and this card will ask us to cease adding extra layers of suffering to the pain. At other times, it will invite us to consider the tenderness we've buried beneath detachment. A third way through it all, the 3 of Swords kicks off the convo between our big old brains and our beating hearts.

What is my usual balance between emotion and analysis, and how are these two realms communicating within me right now?

STREET SIGNS: Write an imaginary dialogue between your head and your heart, and see what they both agree on about your current situation. In NYC, if you're usually a straight-faced subway rider, crack a smile. And if you trend the other way, adopt a more neutral gaze.

The 4 of Swords

→ *The subway doors usher you into the car, just in time. No matter what's happening on the platform or the streets up above, you've managed to stand clear of the closing doors.*

The 4s of the deck are our powerful parentheticals: here to lift us out of the mainstream of life and welcome us into the refuge of retreat. One of the most vacuum-sealed of them all, the 4 of Swords is our magic freeze frame. Whenever we work with this card, we're asked to simply stop it, drop it, and step out of the scene before us. This could mean taking a day off from work, an afternoon away from the needs of a relationship, a few hours away from your phone, or even a second to stop a thought in its tracks. The 4 of Swords shows us that when we give ourselves a break from having to deal, we can reenter when we're good and ready to participate.

> *What do I need to just drop right now, and how can I tend any fears about tapping out?*

STREET SIGNS: Imagine erasing yourself from the current scene, and build trust that you can stage a comeback at any time. In NYC, consciously choose to cut off a phone conversation by losing the signal underground, or let yourself have only the length of your ride to process something before you drop it.

The 5 of Swords

→ *Stuck between stations somewhere in the tunnel, your mind starts to spin. But this is all due to necessary track work. Switch your signals and get ready for the re-route.*

The deck's 5s are seldom fan favorites, but they're never here to harm. Instead, they want to help us understand where we're gripping so we can release our tight hold and find more freedom. In the consciousness raising Swords suit, this 5 wants us to explore our inner wiring and entrenched response patterns. It might come calling when you're ready to reach for a way of being out of habit, even though it makes you feel bad. Or when you're knee-jerking your way through on instinct, without inquiry. Like a chemistry kit, or a Rube Goldberg, the 5 of Swords gifts us the ability to get compassionately curious about our chain reactions.

What kinds of things repeatedly set me off or reel me in, and how can I feel more at choice to engage them?

STREET SIGNS: Map out your greatest "hits" from start to finish, noticing what inspires your strongest reactions, and what kinds of beliefs and feelings they then lead to. In NYC, observe all the stimuli that surround you on the subway, and see how each affects your nervous system.

The 6 of Swords

➜ *You've been riding the rails for so long, you've forgotten that life can be lived aboveground. Suddenly, the train breaks into sunlit song along an elevated stretch of track.*

Each 6 in the tarot lifts us up where we long to belong, and in the circulation of the Swords suit, we're given a vitalizing breath of fresh air. Whenever we work with this card, we're called to recontextualize our current situation. This might mean getting a second opinion—even from within ourselves—or sourcing external input and explicitly asking for assistance or clarification to refine our understanding.

Or it could just be a simple reminder that we don't have to know it all right now: that answers and updates will present along the way. With up-to-the-minute travel times, the 6 of Swords helps us review and renew our route as we ride.

Where might my perspective benefit from some renovation, and how could I invite in a new take?

STREET SIGNS: Write yourself a letter about a life issue from the perspective of another person, or your future self. In NYC, ride along an elevated train line, listen for multiple languages being spoken, and imagine that each was offering different commentary on your situation.

The 7 of Swords

→ *Tapping away on your phone the second the signal returns. Panting for the doors to open and send you sprinting where you long to be. Your mind is already racing toward the next stop.*

The deck's 7s all invite us to consider what we're reaching for and how we're going about getting it. In the space-making Swords suit, we're asked to explore where we might be using distraction to divert from deeper truths. This could mean examining the feelings that an endlessly busy agenda is trying to cover up, or considering the proxy relationships or activities that are standing in for your actual needs. The 7 of Swords doesn't want us to shame ourselves for spinning toward what's sparkly; but it does ask us to focus our attention and hold more empty space for what wants to be uncovered.

Where does my life feel overly full and noisy right now, and what lives beneath the buzz?

STREET SIGNS: Remove one space-filler and see what arises in the blank, whether it's one fewer episode streamed or a canceled meeting that leaves a few unscheduled minutes in your calendar. In NYC, put your phone firmly away until you reach your destination, or let a "showtime" subway performance call your focus into the now.

The 8 of Swords

➜ *The staticky service changes sound like an impenetrable*
   logic puzzle. Trapped in the tangled map, you wonder if
   you'll ever make it through.

All tarot 8s help us increase our surface area: softening us
up so we can participate fully and let more of life in. In the
suit of mental machinations, this 8 might initially find us
feeling bereft of possibilities. But any sensation of binding
is here to be Houdini'd. Whenever we work with this card,
we're asked to first get curious about all the either/ors and
black-and-whites we're believing, and to then begin to
loosen up our linear thinking. When we stop trying to solve
our lives like they were problems with only one solution,
options actually start to spontaneously generate. And our
formerly one-track mind suddenly proliferates with alterna-
tive routes.

> *Where am I feeling trapped in an either/or scenario?*
> *What other possible solutions might arise if I stop trying*
> *to solve it?*

STREET SIGNS: Make a limiting story you're telling yourself into a choose-your-own-adventure, and craft alterna-
tive outcomes. In NYC, master the system's intricacies by
navigating your ride without the use of any maps; or discover the secret subway station at the end of the 6 train.

The 9 of Swords

→ *Jumbo rats, flying roaches, noxious scents, and maybe even*
worse. You've gone so deep underground that each anxiety
amplifies to epic proportions.

The 9s of the deck are where we fold into ourselves like
origami: experiencing our internal intricacies from up close
and personal. In the Swords spin-out suit, our mental inven-
tiveness often starts to go headily hog wild, crafting worst-
case scenarios at breakneck speed. Like an inverse of the 9
of Cups, which calls us to let ourselves wish in the face of
fear, in this card we face fears to uncover the anxious hopes
that exist within our unease. With this 9's help, we not only
find out that our fright nights are part fantasy, but can also
use them to find our way back to the precious human parts
that live beneath the beasts.

What do I fear most in life, and what deeper longings
live beneath these scary stories?

STREET SIGNS: Taking care to tend to your nervous system, play out some worst-case scenarios in your mind and
see where they lead. In NYC, challenge yourself to enter
the "empty car"; lovingly watch rats living their lives on the
tracks; or fearlessly walk on grates aboveground.

The 10 of Swords

➜ *With unlimited MetroCard in hand, you're ready to go the distance. Gliding across nearly 700 miles with the greatest of ease, you run the track.*

The tarot's 10s are the farthest we travel in a given suit, and in the Swords, we're asked to get to know the far reaches of our minds in order to go beyond them. Whenever we work with this card, we're beckoned into our brain's elaborate hope-and-fear factory, and glimpse the extent of our imagination. If we can conjure the wildest of anxieties, we can cook up the dreamiest of dreams. And we can also give our tall tales some truth serum and see where our stories are built on shaky ground. From here, the call of this card becomes even more courageous: to tap our powers as ingenious inventors to actually get out of our own heads.

≡ *When I leave my mind behind, where in my body, spirit, and beyond can I sense what's true?*

STREET SIGNS: Blow your own mind by traveling to a place or engaging in an activity that inspires wordless awe. In NYC, ride from end to end on a given line—or, if you're feeling extra-fit, take the Subway Challenge and shimmy through the entire system on a single swipe.

THE PENTACLES
Pizza Pies

This is the suit where we learn to build competence and stand our ground, gather vital resources, receive the world's sensual richness, and hone our craft with integrity—from dollar cheese slice to artisanal coal-fired pie.

The Ace of Pentacles

➔ *A bread bite to begin your day. A coffee sip to fuel you forward. This city starts with each singular seed and builds toward a BEC on a toasted everything.*

The tarot's Aces are the 101s of their element, offering us the fundamentals. In the earthy Pentacles, this garlic breadstick of an Ace is the first bite before a full meal. When we work with this card, it asks us to show ourselves a sign of faith by choosing a small support to begin whatever we want to build. This could be the first step that helps kick off a new project, or a vital item to inspire you through a charged emotional time. Resourcing ourselves doesn't have to be overly elaborate. Instead, this Ace teaches us that an appetizing amuse-bouche is just as vital as the entrée.

> What one resource could I reach for right now that would help me bolster a new beginning?

STREET SIGNS: Craft a simple packing list of five must-have items—either material or emotional—that you'd place in your survival kit. In NYC, kick off a new cycle of sustenance by enchanting your palate with a previously unexplored cuisine.

The 2 of Pentacles

→ *Like a fish that grows with their tank's contours, this city's tight spaces can tame your tendrils. But you're destined for bigness, and soon start sprawling past your studio's square footage.*

The tarot's 2s are our strength-building exercises in self-reliance, and each one is here to help us start growing in the style that best supports our self-expression. In the Pentacles, we become aware of what we'll need to drop and what we'll need to take on in order to reach our full adult forms. This card often comes through when we begin to naturally become "bigger" than our surroundings—whether it's a relationship we're outgrowing or a little task we can no longer commit to performing because we've got more epic work to do. This 2 asks us to cease sweating the small stuff that no longer fits, and make way for our greatness.

> *What am I already becoming bigger than, and what smallnesses might I need to leave behind?*

STREET SIGNS: Observe things organically breaking free of former constrictions, like plant vines out of pots, or unzipped clothing sloughed off down to the floor. In NYC, secure a deluxe-size granny cart and head to the store to stock up on as much as you can carry.

The 3 of Pentacles

→ *From the deli sandwich slicer to the Michelin-starred chef, everyone in this city serves up their finest dishes for the urban feast.*

The 3s of the deck help us relax our urge to do too much and build trust that we're already inherently good enough. In the material-world realm of the Pentacles suit, this card asks us to embrace the roles that come easiest and just "do" us for a while. Working with it might be an invitation to soften an ambition and just show up to perform your function with maximum finesse. Or, the 3 of Pentacles could be a reminder that your contribution is vital even if you decline to take on anyone else's tasks. By playing to our strengths instead of pushing, we become invaluable players whose skills support the whole team.

What is my role in my own life right now, and how can I relax into it?

STREET SIGNS: Give yourself a metaphorical job title and description, and commit to only taking on what fits it. In NYC, watch restaurant workers during a busy dinner service, each performing their specific tasks, or find a shop that specializes in serving only one item well.

The 4 of Pentacles

→ *Fresh from the store and secure in your street smarts, you've got everything you need stockpiled inside. Firmly fit for city living, you could survive here indefinitely.*

Each tarot 4 helps us rest more deeply within the shape of its element, and gives us an opportunity for secure self-containment. In the body-based Pentacles suit, we're invited to weatherproof our person, deciding where we need to seal up anything that saps our time and resources. It gives us the option to decide who, if anyone, we'll invite inside our den to share them. When we work with this card, we're asked to support ourselves—gathering our inner sources of support close before we extend outward. However, rather than a selfish act of self-absorption, this 4 teaches us that increasing our self-reliance bolsters everyone's capacity to stand on their own two feet.

How can I rely more on myself in this moment, and what am I unavailable to give out?

STREET SIGNS: Take a self-reliance staycation where you build an adult fort inside your home from resources you already have on hand, or enjoy a solo camping trip. In NYC, hole up in your apartment or hotel room for a few days, and order delivery or room service.

The 5 of Pentacles

➜ *You walk the cold streets solo and each window you pass seems warm and toasty inside. Every café table is filled to capacity. You wonder if there's still a place for you here.*

The deck's 5s each carve out empty space so we can examine how we'll fill it. In the earthy Pentacles suit, the gap between what we've got and what we want might send us spinning out into scarcity scaries. It can arise when we've got a hankering for something that's not here and are fearing that we'll never hold it or don't deserve it. Or it could come calling when we're busy believing that someone outside of us is going to magically become our "source" of sustenance. But this card's hollows are never here to deprive us of nourishment. Instead, we can use this 5's space to bolster our belief in our worthiness, and to fill up from the inside out.

≡ *What do I feel desperate for in this moment, and what source do I believe has the power to provide it?*

STREET SIGNS: Examine your wish lists of wants and see which of them you might self-source instead of waiting on an external provider. In NYC, find fun at a free event, uncover treasures at a stoop sale, or enjoy window-shopping without having to purchase.

The 6 of Pentacles

➜ *Just when you think you're out of luck, a lift arrives. Strangers help you drag your suitcase up the stairs. You receive a bonus that covers the rent exactly. The city gives what it can, and you respond in kind.*

The 6s are the tarot's give-and-takes, here to teach us about the exchanges that support existence. In the empty-and-fill of the Pentacles suit, this card carries us beyond the realm of transactional living, into a communal conversation of shared resources without having to run the numbers. This could mean interrupting a pattern in relationships where we only give back exactly what we're given. Or help regulating excess expenditure when we're already emotionally bank-rupt. At its heart, this 6 wants us to cultivate receptivity and generosity of spirit without needing to keep score. We take what we need, and we give what we can.

What am I available to give right now? And what do I need to receive?

STREET SIGNS: Participate in the art of organic exchange at a clothing swap or potluck feast. In NYC, ask for help or offer it to a stranger; or watch seamless transactions occur-ring in a busy marketplace like the Queens Night Market or the Upper West Side's Grand Bazaar.

The 7 of Pentacles

→ *All-night delis serving up 2am delights. Rushes of humans flooding the streets at every hour. Fast-tracked new construction that appears overnight. This town keeps its own time.*

Each tarot 7 is an opportunity to recalibrate our standards. In the Pentacles suit, which asks us how we want to use our precious time on earth, this 7 is our chance to fine-tune our inner clock. Whenever we work with this card, we're invited to challenge external timelines and let our lives evolve at their own, highly personal pace. This might mean questioning where we've internalized assumptions about how far along we "should" be in our journey. Or accepting the finite life span of a project or partnership without feeling like we've failed. When we let this card help us ripen according to our own rhythms, we discover that we're always right on time.

Where am I going "against time" by forcing a slowdown or a speedup, and what is the real rhythm that's wanted?

STREET SIGNS: Develop your own sense of duration by spending a portion of a day where you don't look at the clock. In NYC, face the Union Square Metronome; or engage in an off-hours activity, like visiting a laundromat during the daytime on a weekday, or grocery shopping at midnight.

The 8 of Pentacles

→ *You are shaped by all this steel. Bending your body around*
each concrete corner. Learning the way as you go. These
bricks and mortar are bound to make something out of you.

All 8s are here to do a little work "on" us: teaching us that
strength can also arise through some consensual submis-
sion. In this earthbound 8, we stop trying to manage our
lives, and become apprentices to the process instead.
This might mean releasing attachment to an outcome or
to visions of perfect execution. Or it could ask us to consider where we're caught in a push-and-pull power play and
would benefit from actually giving up and just sliding under.
A card of discipline and discipleship, like wet clay on the
wheel of life, the 8 of Pentacles invites us to enjoy getting
molded by the matter that wants to make more out of us.

> *What does my process look like right now, and how can*
> *I submit to staying in it?*

STREET SIGNS: Enjoy part of an activity mid-process, like
licking cookie batter from a spoon. In NYC, watch bagels
boiling or shaved ice being scraped; packages traveling into
shop basements via conveyor belt; or skateboarders per-
fecting their moves at a skate park.

The 9 of Pentacles

→ *Knowing exactly what you need, you sidle up to the counter and place your order to your exact specifications. This city of customized creations is always happy to serve you.*

The 9 that hews closest to its Major Arcana Hermit progenitor, this card asks us to take all the self-knowledge we've mined from going solo and start using it to treat ourselves better. But this doesn't mean adopting strict green juice regimes or over-correcting when we reach for stimuli that fail to satisfy. Instead, this bespoke process of providing pleasure for the person we are entails honest exchanges with ourselves about our specific tastes. When we start to know our nature, we can actually nourish it. A chance to celebrate the provisions only we can provide, this 9 wants to ensure that we offer ourselves exquisite care.

What tastes define my personal palate, and what do these pleasures reveal about the person I am?

STREET SIGNS: Imagine that you're a guest in your own home and see what you could provide for yourself to make your stay feel the most complete. In NYC, cultivate a "local" spot and treat yourself to a favorite dish; or visit an automat and hand-select your snack from the case.

The 10 of Pentacles

➜ *For those who want it all, this city has it. But the secret to satisfaction doesn't lie in possessing the whole. Instead, it's found in the slice of life that makes it yours.*

The tarot's 10s bring the biggest bounty to the table, and in the Pentacles suit of materiality we may initially find ourselves expecting the plus-sized payout. Yet this 10's greatest gifts are revealed when we start to soothe the story that we can, or should, "have it all." There are things in this life that are here for us—with our name handwritten on their tags—and there are things we'll never touch. This card asks us to make peace with this reality and use it to unlock the limitless riches that lie beneath our feet. No longer grasping, we can make the most of what we've already got and mine more magic from each particle that's present.

How can I soften my quest to "have it all" and instead make more out of what I already possess?

STREET SIGNS: Imagine a portrait of your life as it is right now, and picture how each little piece fits into the frame and serves a particular purpose. In NYC, journey to Mmuseumm or City Reliquary and venerate the divinity in everyday life's extraordinary objects.

The Court Cards ⬂

These cards are symbolic of the many ways of being human and moving through the world. The Court Cards invite us to make like native New Yorkers: to boldly explore our identities, and repossess and express more of our essence.

THE PAGES
Street Snacks

These cards represent our springtime versions of self. They are here to playfully awaken what's been dormant within us, and support the microgreen growth of newness.

The Page of Wands
The Hot Dog

Like the sausage that was elevated to iconic street-snacking status by a New York youth with a pushcart and a dream, the Page of Wands serves up a hot take on our same old self.

As we accumulate life layers, we often lose track of the fact that we're still in the process of daring self-development. When we arrive in this card's energy, we might feel that we just are who we are and are all that we'll become. Or that our superhero shots to have a go at life have run out. But this Page is here to teach us that as long as we're still alive, we still have every chance to become more of ourselves and to rise to whatever the occasion is.

Who am I in this moment, and how can I express a new side of myself?

PEOPLE-WATCHING: Observe the way people introduce themselves for the first time, and let yourself switch up your own intros to fit the moment. In NYC, playfully give it a go by pushing the Astor Place cube; or embrace a silly new version of self by getting your Times Square caricature sketched.

The Page of Cups
The Mister Softee Swirl

Magnetizing kiddos of all ages off playground equipment to await their rainbow-sprinkled turn, the Page of Cups floats its magic melody through the air and gives over its sweetness without measure.

As our hearts go through it all, again and again, we sometimes forget that part of the precious gift of loving is actually our ability to feel in the first place. When this Page comes to visit, we're invited to awaken our tween dream versions of self: those beings who crushed hard on life; penned secret love letters and fantasy fan fiction in their diaries; and became enamored of the sheer range of sensation that was awakening inside them.

What am I feeling in this moment, and how could I have more fun with these feels?

PEOPLE-WATCHING: Witness uninhibited displays of affection and soften your heart with romantic fare. In NYC, check out the performance poetry scene; or commune with the New York Aquarium's moody moon jellyfish and emotive sea lions.

The Page of Swords
The Takeout Container

Adventuring through the streets regardless of the weather, the Page of Swords delivers its ready-to-be-opened spirit straight to your door.

All the cards in the Swords suit ask us to let our perception become more prismlike: they want our understanding of life moments to shift and change according to the light that's currently available. In this youthiest of Swords cards, we're invited to actually get excitedly surprised by what we're learning about our lives. With pencils sharpened and backpacks on, this Page helps us renew our pact with what's still waiting to be discovered.

What am I learning about life in this moment, and
what's surprising my spirit?

PEOPLE-WATCHING: Watch the light of new understanding suddenly come into someone's eyes, or astonish your own consciousness with a trivia game or science program. In NYC, snag a book from a Little Library and open it to a random page.

The Page of Pentacles
The Everything Bagel

A flavor party for the whole body, with more than enough cream cheese to sustain, the Page of Pentacles is the original wonder of this sandwiched world.

Each of the Pages returns us to innocence on the other side of experience: they reawaken our sense of awe in our immediate surroundings. In this Page that's made of material magic, we enter the "please touch" museum of life, and walk the everyday world with increased wonder. This card asks us to cultivate simple and grateful satisfaction for the sensual experience of living here on Planet Earth.

What sensory wonders are available in this moment, and how can I better appreciate them?

PEOPLE-WATCHING: See your same-old world with new eyes by taking a visitor on a tour of your home or town. In NYC, embrace earthly marvels while peeping into the American Museum of Natural History's dioramas, or feeding your senses at an urban farm.

THE KNIGHTS
City Crossings

These cards are the escorts who move and groove us through life's ever-shifting streets: here to help us adapt and respond to the changing circumstances beneath our feet.

The Knight of Wands
The Brooklyn Bridge

From the hot-blooded hustle of Lower Manhattan, to the fast-talking foot of the bridge in Downtown Brooklyn, the Knight of Wands sets us off on one of the city's most spectacular struts.

Each of the Knights asks us to change to meet the moment, and in the self-expressive element of fire we're invited to let taking chances strengthen our self-trust. Whenever we work with this card, we're beckoned to embrace our most spontaneous version of self, and let this risk-ready mode remind us that we can handle whatever happens. When we throw down the gauntlet with this Knight by our side, the challenge brings us back to life.

> *Where am I ready to take a gamble, and how will I handle the consequences?*

PEOPLE-WATCHING: Build your risk tolerance by noticing all of life's mini-roulettes: from sharing an opinion in a meeting, to trying out a new recipe. In NYC, cheer on comics at an improv show or, if you're feeling extra-daring, sign up for a workshop yourself.

The Knight of Cups
The Verrazano Bridge

Across the wide navy Narrows that open into the Atlantic, the Knight of Cups frees us to find our flow and get carried by the current.

There are moments in the tarot that ask us to build our bones and fortify our fortresses. But this Knight reminds us that we are ultimately made of more water than calcium, and are here to increase our power not just by pushing against, but also by learning to go "with." When we work with this card, we're reminded that whether or not we would have chosen our current conditions, we always have the right to relax within them.

> *No matter where I find myself right now, how could I find more flow?*

PEOPLE-WATCHING: Observe birds, or kids in swimmies, bobbing along the surface of shifting waters. In NYC, get playful in one of the city's public pools, like the Olympic-sized Astoria Pool; or kayak your cares away in the waters near Greenpoint, Red Hook, or Staten Island.

The Knight of Swords
The Queensboro Bridge

Channeling every form of transport across its cantilevers from the reaches of Long Island and straight to the heart of the city, the Knight of Swords keeps us lightning-fast for the crossing.

All the tarot's Knights ask us to adapt, and in the Swords' airy energies we're called to levitate just above and explore the many options we have at any moment. When we work with this card, we're always invited to lighten up a little. This could mean finding a touch of humor in an otherwise grave situation, or conjuring your inner chameleon and changing your mind at the last moment. Sprightly in any situation, this Knight nurtures our nimbleness.

> *Where have things gotten too heavy, and how could I lighten up my life?*

PEOPLE-WATCHING: Notice how running errands on a busy day can also keep you feeling buoyant, or wander through a butterfly garden. In NYC, network your way through a Chelsea gallery opening, or get blown in the breeze on a double-decker bus tour.

The Knight of Pentacles
The Brooklyn Promenade

Strolling the elegant esplanade and stopping for a sit-down on a wrought-iron bench, the Knight of Pentacles moves us at the pace, and with the grace, of the body we're in.

The Knights awaken subtle pathways within us, and here in the earthy Pentacles we're asked to explore how our physical forms read and respond to the environment. We can start with a basic body scan, where we pay attention to the nonverbal intel we're receiving about our situation. From this place of psychic physicality, we can then divine how to better "take the shape" of our circumstances and bend our beings toward them without breaking.

> *What info is my body receiving right now? How can I use this intel to help me adapt?*

PEOPLE-WATCHING: Watch animals sensing nonverbally and nestling their bodies into nooks, or humans adapting their dress to meet the weather. In NYC, feel the textured terrain with a pedicab ride; or celebrate environmental remediation along Newtown Creek or the Gowanus Canal.

THE QUEENS
Urban Oases

These cards are our private boudoirs of self before a big night on the town. They ask us to protect our most intimate relationship with the innate power that lives inside us.

The Queen of Wands
The Rainbow Room

With ruby elixir raised high above the glittering city, the Queen of Wands is the inner Rockette who keeps each of us alive and kicking.

In all of the Court Cards, we're asked to "be" rather than "do," and nowhere is this truer than in the quartet of highly internal Queens. The fiery Queen of Wands represents our fundamental vitality: those moments where we feel our fuchsia heart racing and our unequivocal here-ness. Before the passion projects or power moves are pushed ahead, this Queen gives us our lust for life in the first place—and asks only that we Ignite in our own scintillating style.

What makes me feel most alive and connected to my life force?

PEOPLE-WATCHING: Notice the magnetics of someone in a crowded room who inexplicably turns your head and how you, too, possess this power. In NYC, enjoy the relentless flair of the Rockettes; or follow a parade, like Pride or the West Indian American Day Carnival.

The Queen of Cups
The Hall of Ocean Life

Secreted into the inky deep of the world beneath, the Queen of Cups draws us down into the undersea reaches that only we can possess.

The Queens are the furthest inside ourselves we'll ever go, and the Cups' wordless waters represent the most dramatic depth of them all. When we summon this siren, we're asked to explore the secret world of sensitivities that lives within us, and to take responsibility for tending our inner emotional dramas. In this Queen's aquatic energy, we commit to becoming our own closest confidantes, who can hold ourselves close before asking others to hold us.

> *What secret selves and emotional experiences exist within me that are meant for me alone?*

PEOPLE-WATCHING: Imagine the rich inner life of each person you encounter, without having to probe for their actual stories. In NYC, celebrate the covert by slipping into a speakeasy; or share secrets with Grand Central's "whispering gallery."

The Queen of Swords
The Guggenheim

A self-possessed sanctuary for upholding our most serene sight lines and beautiful boundaries, the Queen of Swords encircles us in a spiral of protection.

Each of the Queens helps us find our way through the swirl of sensitivities within, and in the Swords we mix compassion with cool clarity. This Queen wants us to build intimacy by honoring spaciousness. Sometimes this means claiming the contours of our own experience and letting others have theirs, too. It can also mean demarcating safe space within us to keep us shielded from self-harm. However this Queen draws the line, it's always a sign of respect.

Where am I in need of protection? How could creating a boundary help me earn my own respect?

PEOPLE-WATCHING: Observe the edges of things, whether it's a countertop, or receiving or giving a hard "no." In NYC, explore public/private space in Midtown office plaza parks; visit Arbitration Rock on the Brooklyn-Queens border; or draw your own lines in sidewalk chalk.

The Queen of Pentacles
The Greenmarket

Beneath the shiny surfaces of the city's finest eateries, the Queen of Pentacles tends the foundation from farm to table.

The deck's Queens represent the richness of our inner lives, and in the earthy Pentacles we're asked to give ourselves the goodness of ground. When we work with it, this card helps us cultivate internal sources of stability and anchor down into them. Whether it's the sustenance of a sensual act of self-care, or a more metaphorical notion that tethers us during a tough time, this Queen reminds us that we always have the right to take root.

What anchors help me find my internal center? How do I give myself ground?

PEOPLE-WATCHING: Notice foundations and pedestals, and practice sourcing stability by finding your footing on whatever is beneath your feet. In NYC, take root amidst Inwood's ancient geological formations; strike a solid pose beside the Bull of Wall Street; or stretch out on a giant flat rock in a public park.

THE KINGS
High-Rises

These cards are here to help us make, take, and hold space. They ask us to bravely stake our claim and own our footprint, without having to crowd anyone else out.

The King of Wands
Carnegie Hall

Magnanimously spilling its magic straight from the stage, the King of Wands helps us glow in the glory of sharing our gifts with the world.

Each King helps us become a powerful presence in the rooms we enter, and in the fiery Wands we're asked to show up to the party, packing personality presents for all. Working with this card invites us to become more generous with our spirit: sharing the valuable qualities that come to us most naturally, and using them to inspire others. With this King's help, authenticity becomes an act of altruism, and offering ourselves to the audience gives all of us a standing ovation.

What innate gifts do I possess, and how could I share more of them with the world?

PEOPLE-WATCHING: Put a talent on display; enjoy a gift exchange; or trade services with someone. In NYC, book a full Broadway theater experience; start a street show of your own; or unabashedly share your affection for the city with an "I heart" T-shirt.

The King of Cups
The South Street Seaport

Welcoming whatever feast of Fulton Street fishes sails into our port, the King of Cups can hold all of our oceanic emotion and then some.

Each King is a landing spot for our largeness, and in the watery Cups suit our feelings find their most expansive home. We might arrive in this card's energy overwhelmed by our own or another's super-sized sensations that seem to be flooding our lives. But rather than getting sloshed out to sea, this King wants us to create a haven for humanness here on land—letting each emotion that arrives increase our capacity for empathy.

What wants empathy in this moment? How could I become more human?

PEOPLE-WATCHING: Quietly listen to another person's story without feeling like you have to respond to, sort, or fix things. In NYC, embrace your role as a benevolent beacon with a trip to the Little Red Lighthouse; or volunteer at a community-based organization.

The King of Swords
Top of the Rock

High above the street-level drama with a panoramic view of the city and beyond, the King of Swords witnesses the weather with clear-eyed consciousness.

All the Kings embolden our perspective, and in the airy Swords suit we're offered the width of an existential expanse. Within this card's boundless breadth, we're asked to let our response to life become more neutral: viewing our experiences as if they were "just happening," *through* us instead of *to* us. From this observation deck of loving detachment, we can hold maximum space for the events of our precious little lives down below.

Where would it serve me to cultivate some healthy detachment? What parts of my life want more witnessing?

PEOPLE-WATCHING: Meditatively survey your life from a distance and notice what arises; or observe an actual storm from a safe spot. In NYC, gain rooftop access; witness life unfolding within the airy WTC Oculus; or bird-watch in Jamaica Bay or Prospect Park.

The King of Pentacles
Resident Status

You've been on a quest through the city, and now you're ready to come on home. The King of Pentacles gives you the golden key to your piece of high-rise heaven here on earth.

The card that energetically ends our journey through all seventy-eight, this grand-finale King asks us to settle down into our lives and let them grow up around us like vines. No matter what circumstances arise, this card wants us to claim greater comfort and ease within them. Instead of scrambling in search of our tiny sliver of real estate in each situation, with this card's help we learn to make a home wherever we are, and let all of life gather at our feet.

> *How can I get comfier in my current context and let life respond to me, rather than shifting to meet it?*

PEOPLE-WATCHING: Receive visitors from the most comfortable spot in your home or office, instead of traveling out. In NYC, "purchase" a building in the Panorama of the City of New York; or simply sit down on a stoop of your own and settle in for the street show.

About the Author

BESS MATASSA is a Brooklyn-based astrology and tarot reader, teacher, and author who serves up mystical self-inquiry with a side of pop music and pasta sauce. After completing a New York–centric urban geography PhD, she left the campus for the cosmos, first offering her celestial services as "Street Signs" astrological walking tours of NYC neighborhoods. A twenty-year resident of the city, Bess can be spotted sporting hot pink lipstick while strutting the longest streets in each borough, and shimmying to Paula Abdul's "Forever Your Girl" beside the Ruby's jukebox in Coney Island. @bessmatassa bessmatassa.com

Other titles: *The Tarot Almanac* (Sterling, 2023); *The Numinous Cosmic Year: Your Astrological Almanac* (Aster, 2021); *Zodiac Signs: Leo* (Sterling, 2020); *Zodiac Signs: Virgo* (Sterling, 2020); *The Numinous Astro Deck* (Sterling, 2019).

About the Artist

CLARA KIRKPATRICK is an NYC-based illustrator born and raised in the East Village. She received her MFA in Illustration from the School of Visual Arts and has worked with companies like Nike, Google, Five Thirty-Eight, and more.